AF147208

SOUTHDOWN BRISTOL REs

SIMON STANFORD

AMBERLEY

First published 2026

Amberley Publishing
The Hill, Stroud
Gloucestershire, GL5 4EP

www.amberley-books.com

Copyright © Simon Stanford, 2026

The right of Simon Stanford to be identified as
the Author of this work has been asserted in
accordance with the Copyrights, Designs and
Patents Act 1988.

ISBN 978 1 3981 2752 4 (print)
ISBN 978 1 3981 2753 1 (ebook)

All rights reserved. No part of this book may be
reprinted or reproduced or utilised in any form
or by any electronic, mechanical or other means,
now known or hereafter invented, including
photocopying and recording, or in any information
storage or retrieval system, without the permission
in writing from the Publishers.

British Library Cataloguing in Publication Data.
A catalogue record for this book is available from
the British Library.

Origination by Amberley Publishing.
Printed in the UK.

Appointed GPSR EU Representative: Easy Access
System Europe Oü, 16879218
Address: Mustamäe tee 50, 10621, Tallinn, Estonia
Contact Details: gpsr.requests@easproject.com,
+358 40 500 3575

Introduction

Southdown Motor Services, the distinguished operator from the south coast, their buses and coaches easily recognisable in a delightful green and cream, were noted as being a loyal Leyland customer for many years. In 1968 they took delivery of their first Bristol RE buses and further deliveries in 1969 and 1971, plus thirteen inherited with the takeover of Brighton Hove and District, which brought the fleet total to eighty-five.

The first batch were forty-five seaters with Marshall of Cambridge bodywork delivered from April to July in 1968. The second batch seated forty-nine and also had Marshall bodies, and were delivered in 1969 from April onward. These buses were fitted with Gardner engines at the rear and Southdown specified manual gear boxes in both batches. Unpopular with some drivers and on some routes, they were nevertheless part of the history of Southdown and I liked them! Nine were added to the fleet in 1971, again bodied by Marshall. These were semi-automatic with Leyland supplying the engine; these were powerful and easier to drive than their previous counterparts. Three more came in the same year with the more conventional bodywork by Eastern Coachworks. The ones acquired with Brighton Hove and District were Gardner engines, semi-automatic gearboxes and twin-door Eastern Coachworks bodies. The final total of Bristol RE single-deck buses was eighty-five.

In this book I list the batches in detail with a range of photographs accompanied by captions describing the bus and route in as much detail as I can, forming a pictorial history of a type of bus operated by Southdown. Survivors that saw further service following withdrawal after their average twelve years with Southdown are included too. Three known survivors exist and regularly attend shows and rallies in the South East, and they are also featured. I have presented the buses in a random order to give some variety rather than in an encyclopaedia fashion.

SCROLL BADGE

The scroll badge, first introduced during the 1920s, added a super finishing touch to the traditional livery. These were fitted to the front grille on all Bristol RE buses delivered in traditional green and cream.

PPM 210G

Allocated to the western division, Portsmouth, along with most of these former Brighton, Hove and District Bristols, 2210 has a healthy queue of passengers bound for Southsea. Thanks to Travel Lens Photographic.

PPM 210G

2210 was new to Brighton, Hove and District in 1968 and carries twin-door bodywork by Eastern Coach Works. All ten from this batch operated from Portsmouth where 2210 was photographed in September 1981 on its way to Southsea. Those from the batch refurbished by Crosville were painted all-over green as can be seen but minus the white stripe.

PPM 210G

PPM 210G was acquired by Sherrin's of Carhampton, Somerset, *c.* 1982 until passing to Butlins in Minehead about six years later. It was one of the lucky ones to survive in preservation. Bancks Street, Minehead, is the location of 2210 when working the local town service. My thanks to Richard Simons for use of his photo.

PPM 210G
After disposal by Sherrin's, 2210 passed to Butlins in Minehead in the late 1980s and was photographed in use as a courtesy bus around their resort. Note the loss of its registration number.

PPM 210G
2210 had previously been restored in Brighton, Hove and District colours and looks splendid on display at the Netley Bus Rally in 1995. It has recently had a full restoration to National Bus Company green.

PPM 210G
In this view I had given 2210 accommodation at the Southdown PSV premises in Copthorne, *c*. 2012. Engineless and a little down at heel, it was purchased soon after for further preservation, fully restored to National green and now lives in Hampshire.

PPM 210G
Fast forward to May 2024 and beautifully restored 2210 is taking part in an event in Portsmouth to mark the anniversary of limited stop services. Although once preserved in red and cream, it has been painted in all-over green.

NUF 430G
An impressive nine long Bristols were acquired by Heyfordian in Oxfordshire. 430 was numerically the first. Sadly, they had fairly short lives after Southdown with none saved for preservation. Thanks to Nigel Lukowski.

NUF 431G
431 was a Haywards Heath-allocated bus, seen photographed at the bus station, one of five of the longer and higher seating Bristol's regularly seen in the area. It would join several from this batch at Heyfordian after disposal by Southdown.

NUF 431G

431 was one of about ten REs operated in all-white livery mainly for school contracts by Heyfordian Travel in Oxfordshire. Although there is no exact date for this image, it is certainly early 1980s. My thanks to Linda Sposito for allowing use of her late husband Phil's photo.

NUF 431G

Another view of 431 looking a little worse for wear in April 1982 and could have been withdrawn. There seems to be a Gardner engine on the ground, which is ominous. Records of these Bristols after Heyfordian are not plentiful other than most were scrapped. Thanks to Nigel Lukowski.

NUF 434G

434 with Heyfordian based in Oxfordshire. Heyfordian operated about eight of the longer Bristols mainly for school contracts in the early 1980s. All-over white does not suit these buses, or had we become too used to green.

NUF 434G

After her life in Oxfordshire 434 moved north to Warrington in the ownership of a dance troupe. Looking very smart in its non-PSV role, it was photographed by Kevin Ellis in August 1988.

NUF 434G

Owned by the Cromdale Royals, 434 is seen in Stockport, Cheshire, and looks very well cared for and is full of passengers too. My thanks to Graham Ashworth for use of his photo.

NUF 437G

Another Bristol RE to be operated by Heyfordian was 437 for about two years before passing to an operator in High Wycombe. It was then used by a film crew and painted all-over red until *c.* 1984. It was scrapped soon after. Thanks to Nigel Lukowski for use of his photo.

NUF 437G

437 painted in a rather unflattering red and black in use as a film crew bus in the London area, *c.* 1984. I assume it was used to transport crew or provide somewhere for breaks. This was its third and final use before scrapping.

NUF 441G

Service with Heyfordian was short-lived for 441, which sustained severe accident damage and was subsequently scrapped, probably donating some parts for others from this batch. Thanks to Nigel Lukowski for this photo dated May 1982.

NUF 433G

I had travelled to Brighton from Haywards Heath on 433 sometime in 1979 and the terminus was Pool Valley, so I took a quick picture before it returned on the lengthy 170 service to East Grinstead.

NUF 433G

A long-term resident of this depot, 433 stands outside Haywards Heath bus station in March 1980. It has a do not touch sign in the cab area – I do not recall this sign being used. Maybe 433 was poorly and not to be driven.

NUF 433G
433 looking down at heel when seen in Crawley working the rural 161 route. A Haywards Heath-allocated Bristol, this long foty-nine-seat version of the Marshall bodywork ended its days with Southdown allocated to Worthing for a short time.

PPM 201G
2201 was a regular bus on the Haywards Heath local service, along with 2202. Having lived on the route, I was a frequent user. August 1978 is the date of this photo, taken close to the bus station, which was fully operational on this date. John Atkinson.

PPM 202G
A super black-and-white of 2202 making a rare appearance at Uckfield outstation on the 149 service often worked with a Bristol RE. Thanks to Paul Llewellyn.

PPM 203G
Brighton, Hove and District merged with Southdown in 1969 and May 1972 sees 2203 still in red and cream at the Old Steine, Brighton. I would frequently travel on these as a youngster with fond memories.

PPM 204G

A ride around on former Brighton, Hove and District 2204 in 1978. Crawley is the location before a return journey to Brighton. Four of these dual-door Bristols were allocated for a short time to Haywards Heath.

PPM 204G

A year on and 2204 is allocated to Bognor with others from the batch and was photographed by Paul Llewellyn in July 1979. Along with three-quarters of this batch, it too was withdrawn and scrapped in 1982.

PPM 205G
Excuse the street furniture but look at the fuel prices. Portsmouth Bristol with Eastern Coach
Works dual-door body is bound for Southsea. It was withdrawn and scrapped *c.* 1982. Thanks
to Travel Lens Photographic.

PPM 206G
A Portsmouth area photo of 2206 at Hilsea West garage looking very smart, which was the
usual high standard achieved. All the former Brighton, Hove and District were allocated to the
Portsmouth area until dispersed to other garages.

PPM 206G

2206 with Maun of Mansfield, who used it for stage carriage until it passed into preservation and was restored to Brighton, Hove and District red and cream. Thanks to Graham Ashworth for use of his photo.

PPM 206G

This photo taken in July 1989 shows 2206 still in service with Maun of Mansfield and treated to a repaint into their rather garish fleet colours. After being purchased for preservation, it was repainted back to red and cream.

PPM 206G
Back in Sussex, 2206 is on display at one of Amberley Museum's bus shows, looking superb back in Brighton, Hove and District red and cream. The destination display is set for the 37 route commonly worked by these Bristols.

PPM 208G
2208 photographed outside Crowborough garage in August 1975. It spent nearly a year allocated here before leaving this East Sussex location for Hampshire. Crowborough closed in May 1980. Thanks to Paul Llewellyn.

PPM 209G
Former Brighton, Hove and District 2209 is in the Old Steine, Brighton, on its way to Hove station in August 1974. I cannot believe this bus is five years old in this view and I was thirteen.

PPM 209G
This batch of 1968 Bristol REs served Portsmouth well despite their low seating capacity and high standing capacity. 2209 is departing for Southsea, a service in demand looking at the people waiting to board. Thanks to Travel Lens Photographic.

PPM 209G

2209 was in use by the junior kick-start motorcycle team as an office and promotional vehicle attending various events. It is in very much the same condition as when it was sold by Southdown. Seen in Weymouth, March 1984. Thanks to Bob Tarling for use of his photo.

PPM 209G

A rear view of 2209 with the junior kick-start motorcycle team in Weymouth, March 1984. I believe that it continued in use as a caravan of some description, although I have not seen any photos or learned of its location. Thanks to Bob Tarling for use of his photo.

TCD 485J

The Leyland engine Bristol REs once confined to Brighton routes were reallocated and found spread out amongst the Southdown garages. 485 is seen here in Worthing garage in the early 1980s.

TCD 485J

485 parked up in Horsham garage and as it is looking a little tired, it may be delicensed and awaiting disposal. Sadly, this Bristol was not bought for further service and scrapped *c.* 1989 by a dealer.

TCD 486J

Engineering works on the Brighton to London line in February 1983 sees Marshall-bodied 486 at Haywards Heath station providing rail replacement services. There was always an interesting mix of buses allocated to this work.

TCD 486J

486 attended the seventy years of Southdown event along Brighton seafront in June 1985. It is looking very smart and was prepared for the event by your author at Haywards Heath garage. Sadly, 486 was on the disposal list and was sold soon after.

TCD 486J

A stunning black-and-white photo of 486 in Uckfield station yard having worked a 169 service from Haywards Heath. Although 486 was Haywards Heath-allocated at the time of this photo, it is in use at Uckfield. My thanks to Bristol Vintage Bus Group for use of the photo.

TCD 486J

From the batch of ten 1971 forty-five seat REs, 486 was one of my favourites when we were both at Haywards garage. I have numerous memories and photos of it. It was working from Uckfield outstation when this photo was taken.

TCD 486J

Groves of Sheffield made good use of 486 when sold by Southdown. This photo was taken in Sheffield. Sixteen years of sterling service later and it is probably the only surviving RE in an all-over advert. It was reported as scrapped in 1989. Thanks to Graham Ashworth.

TCD 486J

A nearside view of 486 in its all-over advert in Sheffield. A remarkable eighteen years' service for this Bristol and many photographs were taken of this bus including this one by Graham Ashworth.

TCD 486J
In this February 1988 view 486 is seen on a wet and windy day in Yorkshire. At seventeen years old she is looking a little tatty and missing her destination display. A remarkable bus and a missed preservation opportunity as she was scrapped the following year.

NUF 444G
Worthing-allocated 444 is in traditional Southdown green and cream and photographed during the National bus company era as the NBC symbol has been applied. The next stage will be all green with a white stripe.

NUF 444G
On a cold snowy January in 1979 I had just got off the Leyland Leopard behind in Pool Valley, Brighton, and grabbed a quick photo of Worthing-allocated 444 before its departure to Henfield.

NUF 445G
Pictures of 445 with Heyfordian are rare so this early black-and-white photo, albeit poor quality, is a record of its history after Southdown. It was a victim of the scrap man in late 1985.

KUF 210F
Uckfield station yard in August 1978 and 'short Bristol' 210 has finished on the 149 service. Eastbourne's 210 was one of about ten REs allocated to that depot, often ending up at Uckfield outstation. Thanks to John Atkinson for use of his photo.

KUF 211F
Another from the Eastbourne stable is 211, seen leaving East Grinstead on the 180 service to its hometown in August 1979. It was common to see Bristols on this route, which made East Grinstead good for bus spotting. Thanks to John Atkinson for use of his photo.

KUF 211F
KUF 211F sits outside the Southdown garage on Conway Steet in 1979. Often vehicles from other depots would be here for maintenance or on loan to cover vehicle shortages, which made for good bus-spotting territory.

KUF 212F
212 in East Grinstead in July 1979, the same month and year I started at Southdown Haywards Heath, where 212 was allocated. 212 always looked smart – not bad for eleven years old when the photo was taken.

NUF 449G

449, in black and white, was an Eastbourne-allocated Bristol RE with the longer Marshall body, seating forty-nine. It was seen at Haywards Heath bus station waiting to depart for Uckfield, c. 1979.

NUF 449G

Looking a little battle scarred, 449 is at Heyfordian Travel in Oxfordshire in 1982. It was one of ten to join this operator, albeit for a short time. Close examination of the photo reveals an American school bus notice in the bus.

NUF 449G

A late survivor in May 1987, 449 was withdrawn from service after active service in a yard near High Wycombe. The last known operator was Prestwood Travel and 449 no doubt awaits the last journey to the scrap man. Thanks to Steve Foster for use of his photo.

KUF 212F and KUF 221F

The early 1980s saw a cull of vehicles, which included nearly all the Bristol REs. Most went to dealers and many did not see further service. 221 and 212 are visible in this dealer's yard shot. There are unconfirmed reports that 212 did see service for a short time, but 221 did not and was scrapped along with many others. Thanks to Bristol Vintage Bus Group.

Dealer's yard

Another dealer's yard shot. Although poor, it records the history of Southdown and their fleet disposals. This batch of Bristol and Leyland types await their fate, with many of them being scrapped and few seeing further service.

TCD 482J and TCD 485J

A sad sight indeed. 482 and 485 are a shadow of their former selves in this view taken at dealer North's yard in May 1989. These two Bristols that once carried passengers in Sussex and Hampshire now await the dreaded scrap man. My thanks to Mark Hall.

TCD 481J and TCD 490J
The last REs delivered were a batch of ten from 1971. Remarkably, two survive, numerically the first and last: 481 and 490. Beautifully restored, they are on display together at the 2011 Worthing Bus Rally.

NUF 439G
439 became 0439 as an ancillary vehicle in the form of a staff rest room at Uckfield station yard complete with rear-mounted generator. Although its service days ended prematurely, it stayed with Southdown in this role until the late 1980s, when it was scrapped locally.

NUF 439G

Photographed by Paul Llewellyn when wintry conditions were more common, 0439 is seen at the snow-covered Uckfield station yard, January 1985. An auxiliary engine and generator were fitted to provide mains power inside the bus.

NUF 439G

An offside front and later shot of 0439 in Uckfield station yard, *c.* 1988. Several years of standing in the station yard as a crew room has taken its toll and it is looking sad as its useful life is nearing the end.

KUF 211F and KUF 226F
The end of the road for 211 and 226. Delicensed in Eastbourne garage in 1980 awaiting disposal, 211 was reported scrapped soon after whilst 226 had a short reprieve and was used as a play bus at a Sussex school. Thanks to John Atkinson.

KUF 243F and KUF 211F
Eastbourne garage in 1980 and 243 joins other Bristol REs for disposal. Cannibalisation has started with various parts removed to keep others on the road. 243 and 211 were sold to a dealer and subsequently scrapped. Thanks to John Atkinson.

KUF 218F

I recall 218 being allocated to Horsham garage for many years along with others from the batch which were suited to the more rural routes in West Sussex. A rare black-and-white image from my collection shows it at the Carfax.

KUF 218F

218 languishing in a dealer's yard and rapidly deteriorating. I had the opportunity to acquire it for preservation and regretted not doing so. It survived until the early 1990s. An opportunity not fulfilled.

TCD 490J

Seen in 1978, 490 was Haywards Heath-based, and I remember it well. It was allocated to the Burgess Hill town service until it was replaced by Leyland Nationals and was allocated to Portsmouth before disposal. It survives, beautifully restored, in preservation.

TCD 490J

Blue Lake of Chichester ran an interesting and varied fleet including former Southdown Marshall-bodied RE 490 for local bus services. It was well suited to blue and white and was caught by the camera in *c.* 1994.

TCD 490J

490 looks splendid in the blue livery of Blue Lake of Chichester at Southsea Bus Rally in June 1996. It is hard to believe it was twenty-five years old in this view. This Bristol saw much service after withdrawal by Southdown and survives in preservation.

TCD 490J

I was delighted to see preserved 490 at the 2014 Showbus gathering at Duxford. A stunning restoration and finish in Southdown traditional green and cream, it is a credit to the owner. It is hard to believe it was forty-three years old at this time.

KUF 235F

Chichester-allocated 235 is photographed at Compton, a village about 8 miles from its home depot, in April 1979. This is the forty-five-seat Marshall body from this batch of forty and noticeably shorter than the later version.

KUF 235F

Several older vehicles in the fleet were renumbered as fully depreciated vehicles, 235 becoming 3107. This rear view was taken at the Bognor depot in May 1981 and disposal was imminent – no further use was recorded after sale. Thanks to Nigel Lukowski.

KUF 235F

3107, formerly 235, awaiting disposal at Bognor depot in May 1981. This Bristol RE achieved thirteen years' service with Southdown. Sadly, no further service has been recorded after it was sold to a dealer and scrapped. Thanks to Nigel Lukowski.

NUF 447G

Worthing-allocated 447 is on the seafront of its hometown working a 202 service in *c.* 1974. The location is close to the garage, which is still in use by Stagecoach some forty-five years after this picture was taken. It did eventually gain the white stripe to the front.

NUF 447G

Some buses seem to get photographed more than others and 447 is no exception. Although allocated to Worthing, it was caught by the camera at Conway Street, Hove, near to the garage, probably there for maintenance or temporary loan.

NUF 447G 3111

Worthing-allocated 447 with its new fleet number 3111 as a fully depreciated for schools' services in West Sussex, although these renumbered buses did see normal service from time to time.

NUF 447G

447 was renumbered to 3111 *c.* 1980 and is seen here in Worthing garage delicensed in August 1982 awaiting disposal. Despite its smart appearance, 447 sadly didn't find a home after sale and had been scrapped by the end of 1982.

NUF 447G 3111

447 became fleet number 3111 as a fully depreciated vehicle. Disposal was imminent when this rear-view photo was taken in Bognor depot in May 1981. Regrettably, no further use was recorded after sale. Thanks to Nigel Lukowski.

NUF 448G

448 at Lewes bus station working the local 127 service. Normally a semi-automatic would be used. Lewes bus station ceases to exist after closure and now demolition. 448 was withdrawn *c.* 1981, with no further use recorded.

KUF 224F

A black-and-white view of 224 with its new fleet number 3105 in June 1980. Hayling Island depot is the location, in use as storage for withdrawn vehicles. This Bristol, along with 435, saw further service in Ireland.

KUF 224F
224 was one of two Bristols seeing further service with O'Malley's Coaches in Newport, Co. Tipperary, joining the fleet in 1980 and registered 9328 FI. Further details are unconfirmed but it is believed that it was in use until 1985. Thanks to P. M. Photography.

KUF 224F
The rear of 9328 FI, formerly 224, with O'Malley's Coaches, probably on school bus duties in Eire. It looks largely unchanged since its Southdown days. It is believed that it stood in the yard before being scrapped. Thanks to P. M. Photography.

NUF 435G

435, the second Bristol to join O'Malley's Coaches, probably for school contracts, was re-registered 9329 FI. Very little information exists to confirm dates but it had been acquired by 1980 and withdrawn by *c.* 1990. Thanks to P. M. Photography.

NUF 435G

The rear of 435, registered 9329 FI with O'Malley's of Newport, Co. Tipperary. Although the exact location and dates are unknown, it may have been in service longer than 224. My thanks to P. M. Photography.

NUF 438G

Ray Cuff of Piddlehinton in Dorset acquired 438 in 1981 for his rural bus routes. It retained its National Bus Company green, the white stripe being replaced by red. Sadly, accident damage sustained in 1986 resulted in it being scrapped. Thanks to Richard Simons.

PPM 202G

2202, seen at Conway Street, was new to Brighton, Hove and District in 1969. Delivered in their red and cream livery around the time Southdown took over BHD, these twin-door Bristols would become green and white at the beginning of the National Bus Company era.

PPM 203G

Brighton, Hove and District merged with Southdown in 1969 and in May 1972 2203 is still in red and cream at the Old Steine, Brighton. I would frequently travel on these as a youngster with fond memories.

PPM 204G

Brighton station is the location of 2204 in Brighton, Hove and District red and cream before becoming green after the Southdown merger. Another service frequented by the author.

PPM 205G
2205 is turning into Brighton station on service 37, another service frequented by the author many years ago. Thirteen twin-door Bristol REs were purchased by Brighton, Hove and District between 1968 and 1971.

KUF 231F
231 in service with Thomas of Llangadog after sale by Southdown. It was photographed in Carmarthen in June 1980 looking well kept. It stayed in Wales until *c*. 1983 and did see service elsewhere.

KUF 231F

231 was one of the most travelled Bristols after service with Southdown. Following a spell in Wales, it was used as a courtesy bus for Beeches Holiday Park in the Rotherham area. Thanks to Garry Donnelly for use of his photo.

KUF 231F

A nearside view of 231 in Yorkshire as a courtesy bus for Beeches Holiday Park in the Rotherham area in 1985. Looking in reasonable condition but possibly out of use, this was its last known use before scrapping.

KUF 232F

232 was one of a pair of short Bristols in use by independent operator Stanbridge and Crichel in and around Dorset in the 1980s. It was scrapped *c*. 1985, earlier than its sister 239.

KUF 239F

239 was in use with Stanbridge and Crichel in Dorset along with sister 232 in the early to mid-1980s. This photo dates from 1986 and 239 is looking a little worse for wear. 239 was scrapped in 1988, surviving a remarkable twenty years. Thanks to Dave from Flickr.

KUF 239F

In a dark Pevensey Road bus station in Eastbourne on a cold January day in 1979 short Bristol 239, allocated to Eastbourne depot, awaits departure for Uckfield. 239 was sold for further use after disposal.

KUF 240F

A Horsham-allocated short Bristol, 240 is seen at the town centre bus stops called the Carfax about to work a service through to Chichester. After disposal 240 saw many years of further service in Liverpool with Maghull Coaches.

KUF 240F
240, the longest serving former Southdown Bristol RE in service, pictured here with Maghull Coaches of Bootle. It lasted until the late 1990s, an impressive thirty years' service. Thanks to Graham Ashworth.

KUF 241F
This April 1982 photo shows 241 is with Butler of Loughborough, and very much the same as it was with Southdown. Not much further information exists for this Bristol, but I suspect it did not stay long with this operator. Thanks to Joe Gornall for the use of the photo.

TCD 483J

These powerful Leyland-engined Bristols, once confined to the hilly routes in the Brighton area, saw their remaining time with Southdown allocated to depots as required. 483 is seen in between duties at Chichester bus station.

TCD 483J

After disposal by Southdown 483 was used by Cullinan's Coaches in Woodford East, London. The photo was taken *c.* 1987. Looking smart in its new livery as an out-of-town bus, it was sadly reported scrapped *c.* 1988.

TCD 487J

At Haywards Heath in December 1981 487 is heading to Uckfield. Note the gold Southdown fleet names, which were applied to Horsham-allocated buses in connection with the market analysis project in that area. Thanks to Nigel Lukowski.

TCD 487J

Under the ownership of Brighton and Hove Bus and Coach Company, Freshfield Road garage is the location of 487, seen by Nigel Lukowski in March 1986. It would soon be purchased by its new owner, Ambassador Travel, and continue in Sussex. Thanks to Nigel Lukowski.

TCD 487J
Ambassador Travel, based in West Sussex, ran two former Southdown vehicles in the late 1980s. One was 487, here looking superb in brown and cream colours. Both were on display at the Amberley Museum bus show in September 1987.

TCD 487J
All good things come to an end and 487 languishes in the yard of one of the Barnsley breakers, looking very sad indeed and close to destruction. They cannot all be saved but we are fortunate that two of this batch are preserved.

TCD 488J
On loan to Haywards Heath in 1980, 488 is in a very wet and dark East Grinstead awaiting departure to Brighton. It had a short life compared with the other eight from the batch, being scrapped in 1981 following severe accident damage.

TCD 488J
Lewes bus station is the location of ill-fated 488, lost to severe accident damage in 1981, completing barely ten years. Lewes bus station closed completely in 2022 and is due to be demolished at the time of writing.

TCD 489J

A nice shot of 489 at South Parade Pier, Southsea, complete with white stripe before it got repainted in all-over green. Another Bristol not to see further service after withdrawal. Thanks to Adrian Tupper.

TCD 489J

489 was the odd one out from this batch as it is missing its white stripe. Horsham Carfax is the location of this photo taken in January 1986 and 489 is working a school service. It was withdrawn and stored at the closed Horsham garage soon after and scrapped by an Essex dealer in 1988. Thanks to Nigel Lukowski.

TCD 489J

I am pleased to include a photo of 489 at Henfield depot, where it was allocated to school services along with other older vehicles such as Queen Marys and Leopards. My thanks to Paul Llewellyn for use of this photo.

TCD 489J

The end for 489. Seen in an Essex dealer's yard in March 1988, its days are over. It was recorded as scrapped soon after this photo was taken. My thanks to Tim Baker for allowing use.

TCD 489J

A close-up of 489. The photo was taken by Tim Baker in March 1988. A mass cull of older vehicles in the Southdown fleet was taking place including the remaining Bristol REs.

UCD 601J

A black-and-white shot of 601 in traditional green and cream before the renumbering to 491 and a coat of National Bus green and white. Pool Valley, Brighton, is the location, with 601 working the 30 service from Haywards Heath.

UCD 601J
491 at Haywards Heath bus station, 1980. Once allocated to Brighton local services, these three fifty-seat Eastern Coach Works REs saw service at virtually all the Southdown garages as loan buses.

UCD 601J
491 is nearing the end of its Southdown career, and seen here in Pool Valley, Brighton, in February 1986. It did see further service with West Sussex County Council until *c.* 1991 and was scrapped, completing just twenty years' service.

UCD 601J

Another view of 491 at Pool Valley, Brighton, looking a little worse for wear. After many years of sterling service it would be delicensed and stored pending disposal to West Sussex County Council.

UCD 602J

602 in National Bus green and white before becoming 492 in the renumbering at Southdown. It is seen at Pool Valley, Brighton, in October 1974. Its destination was West Dene, a hilly part of Brighton normally worked by these Leyland-engined Bristols.

UCD 602J
492 in Hilsea garage adorned with Waterlooville free bus advertising. Southdown had some competition on their patch and fought back with a Bristol RE – brilliant!

UCD 602J
The author drove 492 with good friend Joe Beckley at Kingscote station on the Bluebell Railway in 1992. 492 was preserved at this time but, regrettably, a year later it was recorded in one of the Barnsley scrapyards.

UCD 602J

492 was preserved and stored at the Horsham Coaches depot on the outskirts of the town and appears to be in good condition. Looks must be deceiving though as it was noted in a Barnsley scrapyard soon after in 1993.

UCD 602J

492 was preserved by Horsham Coaches and used on school contracts when required, a fond reminder of its Southdown days. It remains a mystery to me why its preservation ended abruptly without securing a new owner. Thanks to Graham Ashworth.

UCD 603J

UCD 603J was 493 in the Southdown fleet, one of three fifty-seaters bodied by Eastern Coach Works in 1971. It was seen on one of my many trips to Conway Street garage in 1979 when I worked for Southdown at Haywards Heath.

KUF 235F

In 1980 235 is working the last journey of service 259, photographed by Paul Landymore in East Marden. This Bristol was withdrawn and sold soon after. No further use was recorded and 235 was scrapped.

KUF 236F

Portsmouth-allocated 236 was quite new in this image of it in traditional green and cream livery. One of the shorter forty-five-seat Marshall bodies, it looks superb in this colour scheme, which suited the body style well.

KUF 236F

236 turns red and joins Alder Valley. 236 was acquired *c.* 1974 when this photo was taken in January of that year. The story is that Alder Valley took over the Southdown route and the bus too, the Bristol not looking out of place as the new owner already ran this type.

Bristol badge
The Bristol RE badge. Amongst the Southdown fleet these were fitted to the Eastern Coach Works and 1971 Marshall-bodied buses. Southdown would commonly fit their own name badge particularly on traditionally liveried buses. Thanks to Paul Hoskins.

Marshall badge
A collector's piece of history. A Marshall of Cambridge aluminium badge was fitted to buses with bodywork built by this company. The badge was normally fitted to the inside of the bus along with the body number. The original bus this was fitted to is not known but could have been a Southdown. Thanks to Paul Hoskins.

ECW badge
The ECW badge that was fitted to the fronts of Bristol REs bodied by Eastern Coach Works – only sixteen in the Southdown fleet. This badge is in the hands of a collector with origins unknown. Could it be from a Southdown bus?

KUF 210F

A frontal view of Marshall-bodied 210. Southdown only purchased Marshall bodies from 1968 to 1971, all on Bristol RE chassis. 210 was numerically the first. Photo courtesy of Alan Bishop/ Amberley Museum.

Marshall interior

Marshall sales publicity from 1968 featured the interior of Bristol RE 210. I remember these interiors were well catered for with luggage racks, material-covered seats and ashtrays, probably to Southdown specification. Photo courtesy of Alan Bishop/Amberley Museum.

MARSHALL OMNIBUS DIVISION
AIRPORT WORKS, CAMBRIDGE, ENGLAND

World Famous Metal Bus Bodies

Marshall interior
A second Marshall publicity shot of the interior of 210 from the rear facing the front. Note the ashtrays fitted when smoking was permitted and the notices above warning of overhead racks. Photo courtesy of Alan Bishop/Amberley Museum.

KUF 210F
A rear view of 210. Marshall bodywork was popular with Southdown and not unattractive and nicely finished. Note the advertising which Southdown capitalised on. Photo courtesy of Alan Bishop/Amberley Museum.

KUF 247F
Haywards Heath bus station is the location for 247, working the local service in the late 1970s not long before I joined the company. Sadly, neither the bus station nor the Bristol are with us today.

KUF 247F
Perrymount Road in Haywards Heath opposite the bus station is the location from which 247 is about to depart on the local town service. Another 1979 shot taken before these short Bristols would be sold.

KUF 248F

Passing the entrance to Worthing garage in June 1979 is 248, working a local service in its hometown. It was one of two short Bristol REs to see service for a short time in Loughborough after disposal by Southdown. Thanks to Nigel Lukowski.

KUF 247F and KUF 249F

A super photo of 247 and 249 by Richard Simons, thought to be at Haywards Heath garage where these two were allocated. The change from traditional Southdown to National Bus Company colours is evident here. Thanks to Richard Simons.

EFE 602

Exclusive First Editions produced models of the three fifty-seat ECW-bodied Bristols that were new in 1971. Three were in traditional green and cream and one in National green and white. This one from my collection in green and cream is an early example from 1999.

EFE 603

In 2016 Exclusive First Editions produced UCD 603J in National green and white, with appropriate destination display adding to the fine details included by the model manufacturer – a fine addition to any Southdown model collection.

NUF 430G

A busy Pool Valley, Brighton, in September 1974 and 430 is working service 28 to Lewes. It is in traditional Southdown green and cream, with National Bus Company fleet names telling us that the formation of NBC is here.

NUF 432G

Long Bristol 432 is new in this shot in the traditional green and cream we all associate with Southdown. This livery suited the Marshall body, although it is fair to say it suited all body types. My thanks to Bristol Vintage Bus Group for use of this photo.

NUF 432G

The perfect spot for photos at Haywards Heath bus station and posing for the camera is 432 unusually having worked the local service in Burgess Hill. Sadly, 432 did not see any further use after disposal and was scrapped in 1981. Jeff Jones.

NUF 441G

Haywards Heath-based 441 was a forty-nine-seat Marshall-bodied Bristol, one of several allocated here. This photo was taken by John Atkinson in March 1978 in the West Hoathly and Horsted Keynes part of this route to East Grinstead.

NUF 441G

441 was photographed by John Atkinson as it passes through Horsted Keynes on the lengthy route to Brighton in August 1979. It would be due for withdrawal soon after this date and be sold to Heyfordian Travel in Oxfordshire.

NUF 436G

Another Worthing garage photo and 436 is now a fully depreciated vehicle carrying fleet number 3108 primarily for school services. It worked from Worthing most, if not all, of its time with Southdown.

NUF 443G 3109

Worthing garage is the location of 443, carrying its new fleet number 3109, given to some fully depreciated vehicles for school services. Taken by Nigel Lukowski in July 1981, it was scrapped a year later.

NUF 445G

On a wet and cold December day in 1979 445 is about to collect passengers from Churchill Square, Brighton, and commence the long journey through to Crawley. Thanks to Nigel Lukowski.

TCD 611J

A delightful close-up of 611 in Brighton, Hove and District red and cream colours outside Brighton railway station. Clearly, it is quite new in this view, seen working the 37 service to Kemptown. Thanks to Travel Lens Photographic.

TCD 611J

New to Brighton, Hove and District in September 1970, one of a batch of three, 2211 is waiting to depart from Lewes bus station for Newick. It was withdrawn, sold and scrapped by a dealer in 1982 after just twelve years of service.

TCD 612J
A lovely black-and-white photo of 2212 whilst allocated to Worthing depot, looking very smart indeed. It was another of the batch not to see further service after withdrawal from the Southdown fleet. From the Stan Elliot and Brian Bennett collection.

TCD 612J
Starting life with Brighton, Hove and District in red and cream, 2212 ended its days with Southdown in National Bus Company green and white. It was photographed by Nigel Lukowski in Worthing.

TCD 481J

Pool Valley, Brighton, is the location of 481, seen departing for one of the local routes in Brighton. It is photographed in traditional green and cream and was delivered in this livery in 1971 even though the National Bus Company was formed in 1969.

TCD 481J

Rambler Coaches from Hastings used 481 on their local bus services. The Rambler colour scheme suited the Marshall body well, making it look very smart. 481 had a busy life after Southdown, and it has now retired and preserved.

TCD 481J

481 is one of a pair of preserved 1971 Bristols bodied by Marshall. It is taking part in the Amberley Museum bus show in 2015. It had an active life after service with Southdown with several operators and different liveries.

PPM 205G

Vehicles withdrawn and awaiting disposal during the cull of the early eighties were stored at Hayling Island depot. Amongst many single-decks in store there in August 1982 was 2205, new in 1968. It saw no further service and was scrapped. Nigel Lukowski.

PPM 208G
August 1982 saw many single-deck Bristol REs stored at Hayling Island depot before collection by one of the dealers based in the north of England. 2208 was one and was never used in service again. It was scrapped later that year. Nigel Lukowski.

ECW rears
A wonderful photo taken by Bob Tarling of three Bristol ECW rears at Bognor depot in September 1979. From left to right are 2204, 2213 and 2203, their last known operational depot allocation before disposal and scrapping *c.* 1982.

Haywards Heath bus station
Haywards Heath bus station in September 1982 with delicensed buses in store awaiting collection by a dealer. Bristols 2201, 2202 and 2211 had gone by December of that year, never to see service again. Nigel Lukowski.

KUF 214F
214 was used for a short time by Edmunds Omnibus Services located in the Welsh village of Rassau. It was seen in October 1980 still in National Bus green. It was scrapped around 1983. Thanks to Dave from Flickr.

KUF 233F
Portsmouth-allocated short Bristol 233 at its home depot waiting for its next duty. Southdown buses always looked presentable even in National green and this short Bristol is no exception.

KUF 233F
233 turns yellow and looks striking in this livery of Johnsons in the Manchester area. This photo was taken by Graham Ashworth, who kindly allowed use of this rare image. 233 was reportedly scrapped around 1988.

KUF 244F
Seen in Brighton in September 1977, 244 looks smart in National Bus green and white.
Southdown received forty short Bristol REs in 1968 and over half saw further service after sale.
Unfortunately, 244 was not included.

KUF 246F
Worthing-allocated short Bristol 246 is on the seafront of its hometown working the local
service. A splendid September 1979 photo taken by Nick Bailey. The Marshall-bodied Bristols
carried the National Bus Company green and white rather well.

TCD 482J

482 in traditional livery in a busy Old Steine, Brighton, with 492 and an inspector too. Both Bristols were allocated to Brighton depots in their early lives and are a good comparison of Marshall and Eastern Coach Works bodies. Thanks to P. M. Photography.

KUF 221F

There is no mistaking Horsham Carfax, an interesting photography location where 221 was posing for the camera in May 1974. Still in green and cream, it has had National Bus Company symbols applied.

KUF 226F

A wet, cold and deserted Pool Valley, Brighton, and 226, in traditional green and cream, is departing for Petersfield. Although recorded as scrapped *c.* 1980, 226 was a temporary play bus for a school in Staplefield.

KUF 227F

A delightful scene at Bognor in the late 1970s. 227 is leaving for North Bersted, close to its hometown. Bognor was a bus enthusiasts' paradise with a wide range of buses and coaches and a healthy allocation of Bristol REs.

UCD 602J
A black-and-white shot of 492 in a very wet High Hurstwood, East Sussex, making its way to Uckfield working service 149. Thanks to Paul Llewellyn, who took this photo in March 1984 before 492 was transferred to the Portsmouth area.

UCD 602J
A little over a year later from the previous photo and 492 is in Hampshire. Photographed by Paul Llewellyn in September 1985, 492 is turning into Havant bus station.

UCD 603J
Back to East Sussex and 493 is working from Uckfield depot, where it was photographed by Paul Llewellyn in November 1984 at Fairwarp working the 149 service. 493 did not see further use after withdrawal and was reported scrapped *c*. 1986.

UCD 603J
I cannot resist a rear-end photo and have many in my collection. Paul Llewellyn caught 493 with his camera in November 1984 in Chillies Lane, High Hurstwood.

KUF 215F
215 is entering Pool Valley bus station from the Old Steine, Brighton. This is a super black-and-white view not only of the Bristol but a reminder of the buses and buildings of Southdown in the 1960s and 1970s.

UCD 601J and UCD 602J
This is one of my favourite photos and features 491 and 492 in Worthing garage in May 1981. These three Eastern Coach Works-bodied fifty-seaters would be used at most of the Southdown depots as required.

NUF 430G
A magnificent photo of Pool Valley, Brighton, in May 1971. 430 is next to a Queen Mary. Both buses look resplendent in Southdown traditional green and cream. My thanks to Paul Jenkins.

TCD 485J
A lovely shot of Brighton-allocated 485 in traditional green and cream colours at the Old Steine, Brighton, in May 1971. Look at the amazing architecture whilst also admiring the bus. My thanks to Paul Jenkins.

NUF 437G

437 in a darkened Worthing garage. Like sister 436, it spent a lot of its Southdown career on the south coast at Worthing until withdrawal and was bought by Heyfordian in Oxfordshire.

PPM 210G

We finish where we started and beautifully restored 2210 is on display at Stokes Bay Bus Show in August 2019 with Bristol VR 583, also restored to a high standard. Thanks to Martyn Davies.

KUF 211F

Freshly back from a repaint, Eastbourne-allocated 211 is looking rather smart when I saw her parked in the garage. These were not ideal photo conditions in a gloomy bus garage in the 1970s when camera equipment was somewhat basic.

TCD 486J

A colourful shot of 486 approaching the Old Steine, Brighton. I would guess that 486 could be a contender for the most photographed Bristol RE probably due to the fact she worked at some time from most of Southdown's depots and saw service after disposal. Thanks to Travel Lens Photographic.

KUF 233F

Another photo of 233 in the Oldham area in a very distinctive yellow livery sporting a Gardner badge. It is believed she had three owners in this area after sale by Southdown. Unfortunately, she did not survive beyond 1988. Thanks to Graham Ashworth.

KUF 228F

One of my favourite Bristol RE photos, 228 is at Uckfield out station *c.* 1979 having worked a Tunbridge Wells to Brighton 729 service. Another one from this batch not to see further service after sale.

KUF 229F

Another ride around for me in the 1970s, this time to Horsham and waiting at the Carfax to travel back home to Haywards Heath on Horsham-allocated 229, one of several 'short' Bristols based here.

TCD 486J
The ever-popular 486 working the short distance Centrebus service from Brighton station to the Churchill Square shopping centre. A black-and-white image from the Brian Bennett and Stan Elliot collection.

UCD 602J
Still carrying fleet number 602 in the fleet prior to the delivery of Bristol VR 602 in September 1977 when this Bristol RE would become 492. 602 is seen at Churchill Square Brighton working the short Centrebus service. From the Brian Bennett and Stan Elliot collection.

Appendix
The Southdown Bristol REs Fleet

210–249. KUF 210F–KUF 249F Bristol RESL6G. Marshall B45F bodywork new in 1968. Total forty.

430–449. NUF 430G–NUF 449G Bristol RELL6G. Marshall B49F bodywork new in 1969. Total twenty.

481–490. TCD 481J–TCD 490J Bristol RESL6L. Marshall B45F bodywork new in 1970. Total ten.

491–493. UCD 601J–UCD 603J Bristol RELL6L ECW B50F bodywork new in 1971. Total 3. Originally carried fleet numbers 601–603.

2201–2210. PPM 201G–PPM 210G Bristol RESL6G ECW B35+27D bodywork new in 1968. Total ten.

2211/2212/2213. TCD 611/612/600J Bristol RESL6G ECW B37+28D bodywork new in 1970. Total three.

Acknowledgements

Most of the photographs included in this pictorial history of the Bristol REs owned and operated by Southdown Motor Services are from my own collection spanning over forty-five years.

To enable me to include some rare images, friends and fellow enthusiasts have been willing to help, particularly with some images of these Bristols that operated in other parts of the country after disposal by Southdown.

My sincere thanks to the following: my good friends Paul Llewellyn and Nigel Lukowski, Richard Simons, Graham Ashworth, John Atkinson, Bob Tarling, Steve Foster, Mark Hall, The Bristol Vintage Bus Group, Phil Moth from P. M. Photography, Jeff Jones, Travel Lens Photographic, Kevin Ellis, Garry Donnely, Joe Gornall, Adrian Tupper, Tim Baker, Paul Landymore, Paul Hoskins, Amberley Museum for use of the late Alan Bishop's photos, Nick Bailey, Martyn Davies, Stan Elliot and Brian Bennett collection and Paul Jenkins.

My thanks to Linda Sposito for the use of her late husband Phil's photo of NUF 431G.

My thanks to Amberley Museum for the use of photos of KUF 210F donated to them from the estate of the late Alan Bishop, who worked for Southdown as a manager and inspector at Chichester and Worthing garages.

I hope I have not forgotten anyone; apologies if I have.